GIFT OF
LIFE AND LOVE

Love, Marriage
and Natural Fertility Regulation

by
John J. Billings

To my Parents

*All booklets are published thanks to the
generous support of the members of the
Catholic Truth Society*

CATHOLIC TRUTH SOCIETY
PUBLISHERS TO THE HOLY SEE

CONTENTS

From the Foreword to 1987 Edition

This booklet is not simply a useful introduction to the Ovulation Method. Although it includes accurate advice on how to postpone or achieve pregnancy, it goes much further. *The Gift of Life and Love* reveals the wisdom which is behind any natural way of responsible parenthood. Always, we are to keep life and love together, never separating these two dimensions of the covenant partnership of holy marriage. This is the wisdom within the teaching of Pope Paul VI in *Humanae Vitae* 12, developed further by Pope John Paul II in *Familiaris Consortio* 28-35.

May all who read this booklet place themselves in the Presence of God, seeking His guidance. His enlightenment. May couples find in it a way forward to a deeper love, to shared decisions, mutual respect and openness to one another. May they come to understand their fruitfulness and so be able to return that gift of life to God. May they build better families and so make visible in their lives the sacrament of spousal love and that divine self-giving which says 'forever'.

Edouard Cardinal Gagnon, P.S.S.

(Past President, Pontifical Council for the Family Rome: Nativity of Our Lady, September 8, 1987.)

From the Foreword to 1997 Edition

In this excellent introduction to the natural regulation of fertility, Dr. John Billings discusses one of the natural ways of achieving or postponing pregnancy. At the same time he sets out the wise philosophy of married life and love derived from the teaching of Pope Paul VI in *Humanae Vitae* and Pope John Paul II in *Familiaris Consortio*.

In proclaiming the Gospel of Life in the Encyclical Letter *Evangelium Vitae*, Pope John Paul II says: "The work of educating in the service of life involves the *training of married couples in responsible procreation*. In its true meaning, responsible procreation requires couples to be obedient to the Lord's call and to act as faithful interpreters of his plan." (*EV* 97). When couples choose the natural methods for serious reasons and in respect for the moral law, they co-operate with the Lord of Life, who is the Centre and Source of the Gospel of Life.

Alfonso Cardinal Lopez Trujillo,

(President, Pontifical Council for the Family
Rome: Annunciation of the Lord, March 25, 1996.)

Introduction

"The Gift of Life and Love" is especially directed towards older children and young adults, especially those who are beginning to think about marriage, or perhaps are already married. It may also help Priests and Parents whose love for these younger people makes them want to help them to make wise choices, good plans for the future and to recognise that a happy marriage succeeds by being built up every day. Love is a wonderful emotion as we all recognise, but it is important for us to perceive that true love is more importantly an act of the will, essentially manifested by promoting the welfare of the beloved person.

It is important to understand that my dear wife Evelyn and myself did not create or invent the Billings Ovulation Method. We did however discover it and studied it to allow for the formulation of appropriate guidelines to enable the method to be used successfully for the achievement or the postponement of pregnancy. There is no method, natural or artificial, that is more effective in either of those areas than is the Billings Ovulation Method.

The Billings Ovulation Method is based on the reproductive physiology shared by all women. It is because the method promotes co-operation and understanding between the husband and wife, and the generosity which helps them to accept the gentle discipline of the method as a manifestation of their love, that the couple grows in love for each other, in love for their fertility, and therefore in love for their children even before those children are conceived.

John and Evelyn Billings,
Kew, Australia, April 2002.

Love and Marriage

The philosophical ideals of married love and happy family life can be perceived by many persons who are not Christians. But Christ in his own words, and through his Church, has given us an even more exalted view of married love, and has made marriage a sacrament, a means of grace. Christians have a special obligation to give witness to the world that their view of marriage is true, so that more and more will strive to maintain the integrity of marriage and the purity of love. Somehow, the message is not getting through; perhaps we ourselves do not understand it well enough; perhaps we are not proclaiming it loudly enough and with conviction; I do not believe that the world is merely refusing to listen.

Marriage is Creative

The husband and wife obtain in marriage the privilege of the closest act of human co-operation with God and His creative power. After our creation and our redemption, this share in the creation of new human life is our most precious gift. An act of love occurring in time exerts an effect throughout eternity when it is generative of a new person, who has an immortal soul and whose destiny it is to spend eternity with God. The loving sexual union of the husband and wife has become an echo of the Blessed

Trinity itself where the Holy Spirit is generated by the mutual love of the Father and the Son.

One sees in the animal kingdom that the primary purpose of the sexual union is the reproduction of the species. In human generation many prefer to speak of procreation rather than reproduction, in order to emphasise the uniqueness of each individual human being.

In the human relationship, the act of coitus also gives physical expression to a continuing state of the spiritual and psychological union of two persons who have publicly committed themselves to a covenant whereby there will be henceforth not two lives but one. Here one sees the nuptial significance of the body, as Pope John Paul II has reminded us, the complementarity of the sexes providing for a union of love that permeates all levels of human existence, enabling man and woman to grow together and to care properly for their children. Life and love have now become inseparably united, the faithful and fruitful love between the spouses reflecting the union of love between Christ and the Church. Even those without religious faith understand the kind of love which reflects the true meaning of the word - "the real thing" - which is a love that binds a man and woman together forever, such that they long to live out a pledge of selfless endeavour in the service of the beloved.

Love that does not include sacrifice is incomplete. Sacrifice or pain joyously embraced for the sake of the loved one is at the heart of the mystery of love. This helps us to understand why the happiness of the physical sexual union should at times be set aside, despite great longing for it, for the sake of the other person, perhaps by each for the sake of the other and for their children. As Pope Paul VI told us: "This discipline which is proper to the purity of married couples, far from harming conjugal love, rather confers on it a higher human value... Such discipline bestows upon family life fruits of serenity and peace, and facilitates the solution of other problems; it favours attention to one's spouse, helps both parties to drive out selfishness, the enemy of true love; and deepens their sense of responsibility."[1]

Pope John Paul II revealed his profound concern for the welfare of the family even before his election to the Papacy. "Marriage and the family", he said, "are invariably at the root of all the affairs of man and society. Although it is, one might say, a most private concern, an affair of two persons, of husband and wife, and of the smallest social group, which they form together with their children, yet the fate of nations and continents, of humanity and of the Church depends upon it."[2]

Shortly after his election he published an Encyclical "*Redeemer of Man*" *(Redemptor Hominis)* in which he said: "Man cannot live without love. He remains a being that is incomprehensible for himself, his life is senseless if love is not revealed to him, if he does not encounter love, if he does not experience it and make it his own, if he does not participate intimately in it" *(Chapter 2, section 10)*.

A child learns to love by being loved, and he finds his first experience of love within the family. He gradually discovers what love means and comes to see that it was there even before he became aware of it. He was born into the world helpless, and both his body and his personality were able to reach maturity only by receiving the nourishment which they required.

The marriage Covenant

When a man and a woman make a considered commitment to one another in marriage, with love and a good intention in their minds, they can be sure that they are fulfilling the destiny which is appropriate to them within God's Providence. The words of Ronald Knox are appropriately addressed to every couple at the time of their marriage: "Like swimmers carried away by a silent undertow that is too strong for them, you are being swept into the current of that Divine love which reaches beyond time and sense; united, beyond your knowing, with that Divine will which made you for one another."[3]

We cannot command ourselves always to feel affection, but we can command our wills to love. When the husband and wife enter into marriage they take upon themselves two serious responsibilities - there is the responsibility involved in the gift of oneself to the spouse, and the acceptance of the gift of the other is a separate responsibility which helps to identify and at the same time enlarge the first. The responsibility of the married person is to work in fidelity to the conjugal love in order to bring the other and oneself to perfection. "The bride and bridegroom promise one another union, love and conjugal faithfulness. On this foundation rests that spiritual edifice, the construction of which can never cease... They must renew this oath daily in their hearts and sometimes recall it also in words."[2]

Fertility is a vital element of the human organism. The biological differences which exist between male and female irrevocably determine their earthly roles within the whole of humanity, providing for a creative partnership between men and women which extends beyond genital communication into the whole meaning of their sexuality. A man is a man-person, and a woman is a woman-person. In marriage the fertility of the husband and the wife bind themselves to each other and to their children, and an *intended* removal of the fertility of one or both of them separates them from each other and from their children. It is the knowledge that they share a power by which a new human life may be brought into existence that establishes and perpetuates a special, exclusive bond which gives meaning to the whole concept of the family. It is a tragedy of modern times that so many men and women have been willing, even eager, to destroy their fertility, that a husband or wife will not grant to the other, even to themselves, an acceptance that includes acceptance of their fertility. These "modern eunuchs", as they have been called, reflect a mortal sickness of the mind, an attitude which has produced in our own time an anti-child society.

The *Catechism of the Catholic Church* has many beautiful statements regarding the nobility of Christian marriage and the Christian family. We sometimes forget that it was marriage that formed the first social unit to appear; the family which has remained of fundamental importance in almost every culture that has existed in human history. Firm adherence to the traditional Christian philosophy regarding conjugal love, family life, the procreation of children and the responsible and prudent regulation of births, is what is needed to generate love, truth, peace, happiness and unselfish care of those who are disadvantaged in human society. (See Appendix, Page 74-77).

Spirit over Matter

Preoccupation with the theory of evolution may distort one's concept of love. Much of what is now written about sexuality reflects an assessment of human beings as mere "super-beasts". Their various animal instincts are thought to demand gratification for sound physical and mental health, with inevitable corollaries of sterilisation for eugenic purposes, artificial insemination, amniocentesis for the identification and destruction of children likely to be handicapped, euthanasia and so on.

On another occasion John Paul II said that man "must rediscover his authentic kingship over the world and the fundamental meaning of this dominion of man over the visible world consists in the priority of ethics over technology, the pre-eminence of people over things, and the superiority of spirit over matter."[4]

One can acknowledge the insight provided by advances in our knowledge of human psychology, without being deceived by the excessive claims of some psychologists. Pope John Paul II insists upon the fundamental Christian teaching that man is normally capable of making responsible decisions because he has free will. In fact this is the only genuine freedom for the human individual, a freedom to make decisions in regard to actions which have moral significance. It is because men and women are free that they are capable of entering into binding commitments, and this proposition lies at the very foundation of the civil law of contracts which will certainly not permit the normal person to abrogate a contract unless he can positively prove coercion or diminished mental capacity. This is not to underestimate the force of social, economic and political pressures which limit human autonomy.

In his weekly audiences during 1980-81 Pope John Paul II pointed out that if man in his relationship with woman considers her only as an object to gain possession of and not as a gift, he condemns himself thereby to become also for her an object of appropriation, and not a gift. The "belonging" arising out of the gift is altogether different from the belonging of appropriation. Lust in general - and the lust of the body in particular - attacks precisely the "sincere giving." It deprives the human being of the dignity of giving which is expressed by the body through femininity and masculinity, wherein the husband and wife bring each other more completely to the image of God.

A Perpetual Surrender

In making men and women complementary to each other and creating the physical union of marriage, God intended that it should express this idea. They are one flesh, and sexual intercourse symbolises a perpetual surrender and sharing of their whole lives thereafter. It is when the physical act gives expression to this continuing attitude of mental unity and love that sex finds its fulfilment, and emotional and physical contentment become most exquisite. Here are joy and pleasure that the promiscuous individual has never experienced and scarcely understands.

The essence of love is generosity. St Thomas Aquinas, following Aristotle (as had St Augustine), taught that love implies the intention of bringing about the greatest possible happiness of the person loved.[5] The love which is totally generous nourishes and enriches itself as well as the personalities of the husband and wife, whereas "a love which is all of the body, not of the soul, soon becomes a thing of yesterday."[3] True love is like the jar of oil that never fails.

Love depends upon reverence, and the purest love flows from reverence for God, with reverence then for the work of His hands and the object of His love. Love is not blind, but looks deeply into the other to find a creature made in the image of God. When the husband says, "With my body I thee worship", he is acknowledging the revelation of God's nature in the woman he is marrying.

To Love and be Loved in return

Most of us can recognise in ourselves and see in others the basic urge to receive and to give love; this is essential for the full development of the human personality. One sees a number of unhappy individuals who have grown into adult life bitter and frustrated, without ever having learned of love, because they have been unloved in the world and have never been taught about the God who loves them. It is another creative aspect of married love that the spouses complete and perfect each other and create an atmosphere within the family where the child finds security and happiness.

Love is sanctifying because it enables the soul to find the Creator who is Love itself. "How can the man who has no love have any knowledge of God, since God is love?"[6]

Heaven is love that endures and there is no better image of Heaven on earth than the love of a husband and wife for each other. "If we love one another, then we have God dwelling in us, and the love of God has reached its full growth in our lives."[7] Henceforth, every incident of the life together is hallowed by His presence, as at Nazareth. "Where there are charity and love, there the God of Love abides."[8] And two Guardian Angels have joined in a common task.

The physical union between husband and wife is a loving, joyful expression of their giving themselves to one another as long as they live. This love will find expression in many other ways because love should be constantly expressed and demonstrated and there will be times when sexual union is not possible. There are times when it is abstinence from sexual union which is the demonstration of love. And they look forward to the day, after the temporary separation by death, when they will join their hands again in the peace of Heaven.

The lives of those who have chosen virginity for the love of God can be a source of inspiration and strength, "the witness of the priest who, in order to be a pastor with Christ and in His name, in order to be unreservedly at the service of His brothers, offers himself entirely to the One who has chosen him, to the One who can and must fill his life."[9] The purest and most generous love in marriage springs from a selfless love of God. Pope Paul VI also holds up to us the example of St Joseph with his "total commitment to Mary, the elect of all the women on earth and of history."[10]

Love founded in God

Having created marriage as a triangular partnership of creative activity in the first instance, God endowed the physical union with the power to express and increase the love of the partners for one another. Thenceforth, these purposes of marriage and sexual union become indivisible, so that in begetting children the parents manifest their love, and in manifesting their love they themselves never exclude any creative potential with which God has endowed the act of intercourse at that time. Marriage is for the good of the offspring, who are begotten and nourished (*educare*) by their parents' love. In this completeness, the progress of the husband and of the wife to perfection is leavened by the Sacrament they have administered to one another, and their marriage will take them to Heaven.

Pope Paul VI has reminded us that "Conjugal love reveals its true nature and nobility when it is considered in its supreme origin, God, who is Love, the Father, from whom every family in heaven and on earth is named."[11] He defined the characteristic marks and demands of conjugal love: that it is "*fully human*, that is to say, of the senses and of the spirit at the same time"; that it is "*total*"; that it is "*faithful* and *exclusive* unto death"; and that it is "*fecund.*" Conjugal love is "an act of the free will, intended to endure and to grow by means of the joys and sorrows of daily life, in such a way that the husband and wife become one only heart and one only soul, and together attain their human perfection."

When St Paul[12] told us that the husband is head of his wife, he put forward the example of Christ as head of his Church, indicating the role of the husband as devoted friend and protector. Many men have never learned the truth of this saying of St Paul, although, generally speaking, women understand it very well. The husband is to be the head of the family, he is the protector of his wife in all that concerns her well-being, her rest and recreation, her emotional stability, in the provision of a home and material necessities and comforts; he is the bulwark against the evils and dangers of the world. He needs to develop the conviction that she now is a gift to him, it is now his right and obligation to guard and cherish her, and that he intends to do so no matter what anyone, even she herself, may say.

Masculine and Feminine

The husband and wife should understand that marriage is essentially different from any sort of business contract. Marriage is a partnership not of equals, but of two persons who are physically and emotionally different and who have different contributions to make to the partnership. Sometimes a woman may complain that the only time her husband speaks of love to her is when he wishes to have sexual intercourse. This denotes his failure to appreciate that a wife feels secure in her husband's love only when she is reminded and reassured of it daily.

A husband who lacks the wit to discern this fact may be indignant when reproached, insisting that his temperance, fidelity and industry on behalf of the family are sufficient to convince "any fool" of his love. They are enough to convince "any fool" of a man, but a woman's nature needs assurance of another kind. She needs words and gestures of affection, little demonstrations that persuade her that in all her activities she is bathed in a fountain of love, and that some day her loving guardian will present her to God "without spot or wrinkle or any such thing."[13] In one of the beautiful poems which G. K. Chesterton wrote to his wife, he expressed this idea in the following words: -

"You cannot guess
How I shall flaunt before God's knights
The triumph of my own princess...
I swear it shall be mine alone
To tell your tale before the throne."

What St Paul is saying is not appropriate only to a particular historical setting, nor related to the status of women in society, but has permanent application because of its insight into the essential differences in the masculine and feminine natures.

In the normal course of family life, the children are at first in direct control of their mother and identify themselves with her. She provides the care and discipline which establish them in emotional security. The mother suffers physical and emotional depletion in these tasks and her husband stands in the same relationship to her as she does to the children. If he does not provide the love and security that she needs she will be depleted from both sides and is in danger of physical and mental breakdown.

Identifying themselves with the mother, the children react to her emotions, copy and follow them. As the children become older they develop a more personal relationship with their father. To the growing girl the father is her first man, which means that she recognises him as the person who is providing the authoritative care of the family for which she will look ultimately to her own husband. The boy, even by the time he is three or four years old, begins to learn to identify himself with his father and to imitate him. In adolescence the boys develop an affectionate "mateship" with their fathers and it is respect for his authority and character that helps them to become good citizens.

Some Hazards

A good deal of sexual frigidity in women springs from a background of a disturbed family life during childhood, and particularly a failure of the father to fill his proper role. In young men homosexuality may appear when they have been unable to learn respect for their father, many cases of homosexuality arising in a family where the mother is aggressive and domineering, whilst the father is meek and submissive. The problem may be that of a father who is absent from home too much.

Another problem that can arise despite the relative prosperity of citizens, is that of the father who works long hours of overtime at night and at weekends. He is resentful if he is accused of being a workaholic, claiming that he is working so hard only to give his family security, not realising that no bank balance, however large, can make up to a family for the absence of the husband and father. Divorce statistics show a striking frequency amongst the husbands in occupations which cause long absence from home. It is possible, of course, for the man to maintain his position in the family even when he is unavoidably absent, by sharing those elements of his employment which the family can understand and has a right to know.

The husband's role was beautifully expressed by the twelfth-century poet who said "Woman was not taken from man's head, for she was never meant to rule, nor from his feet to be his slave, but from his side to walk beside him, from beneath his arm to be protected by him, from near his heart that he might love and cherish her."[14]

Understanding differences

Difficulties in the development of sexual harmony are commonly the result of a failure to appreciate the importance of this proper relationship of the husband and wife to each other, and their difference in physical and emotional reactions.

It is well known that physical arousal comes easily and quickly to a man; the adolescent boy learns this too. Part of the development of his manly character is the achievement of control of physical reactions which may come so quickly as to catch him unawares. A man's emotional responses can be slower to develop and the whole act of sexual intercourse may occur without his having experienced more than physical satisfaction. When this is so he will sense the deprivation of that emotional happiness which God intended he should enjoy.

On the other hand women are more easily aroused emotionally, whilst the development of physical responsiveness is not only slower but will depend upon a preceding emotional arousal, turning their minds towards their husbands in a state of love.

Physical stimulation by the husband designed to produce sexual arousal, may cause emotional upset, especially if introduced too early into the total content of sexual intercourse. The husband should first concentrate his wife's mind on the constancy and sincerity of his love for her, and this would be more easily accomplished if he has been in the habit of showing it. Once she is emotionally and physically ready, and has a husband who is worthy of physical loving, she will become more responsive and with the beauty of her body give him a full measure of emotional and physical contentment.

Happy sexual loving

Whilst there may be a happy and loving relationship in a marriage where complete sexual harmony has never been established, and whilst the frequency of this physical expression of love is very variable, it can be said that in the majority of happy marriages sexual loving is a source of great happiness. This is not only because it reflects a deeper and more lasting union, but also because happy sexual loving intensifies and increases the bond between the husband and wife. The love continues to be creative in establishing an atmosphere of serenity most conducive to the full development of the personalities of the children. A great deal of nervous and mental ill-health and behaviour disorders in children and adults can be traced to early environmental influences arising from disturbances and breakdown of family life. As the poet has put it:-

"In ancient shadows and twilights
Where childhood had strayed,
The world's great sorrows were born,
And its heroes were made.
In the lost boyhood of Judas
Christ was betrayed."[15]

RESPONSIBLE PARENTHOOD

The Christian concept of marriage is not to be regarded as a remote ideal. There is no snobbishness in Christianity. To hold the view that marital chastity is a level of virtue to be attained only by those of exceptional strength of character or unusual piety is to underestimate the generality of mankind. And the more the Christian view is propounded with the serious intention of inviting its universal application, the more chance there is of a consensus of opinion that will limit the errors and follies which come from clouding of the intellect or weakness of the will. As the Archangel Raphael said, "The fiend has power over such as go about their marrying with all thought of God shut out of their hearts and minds."[16]

Generosity

The essence of love, and therefore of responsible parenthood, is total generosity. All the great saints of the Church have exhorted us as did Ignatius of Loyola, to "give and not to count the cost." True happiness can be achieved only by loving generously. The person who says plaintively, "Why should I have to give all the time?" has not understood the paradox of which Francis of Assisi reminds us, "It is in giving that we receive." The privilege of sharing in the creation of human life does not require much reflection for the wonder of it to become apparent. The husband and wife who remember and understand that marriage involves a total gift of self to the spouse, including the exclusive gift of their fertility, rejoice when they act in a partnership of creation which brings into existence a human personality whose immortality will allow him to enjoy the happiness of the knowledge of God beyond all time. The liberty provided by a technique of family planning which is secure, harmless and morally lawful permits us to become the responsible builders of a sane society on earth and of a heavenly kingdom.

Christians understand therefore that children are the supreme gift of marriage, contributing to the material welfare as well as to the eternal destiny of their parents. Those parents who, in response to a careful decision of their conscience, appropriate to the opportunities provided by their particular circumstances, confidently and generously have and educate a large family are worthy of all the economic support they require, not as a gratuitous concession but as a just contribution from a grateful society. In an address to the Family Front, on 26 November, 1951, Pope Pius XII, after reminding his listeners that the primary function of matrimony is to be at the service of life, went on to say, "...our Fatherly gratitude goes to those generous mothers and fathers who for love of God and trust in Him courageously raise a large family"[16a].

Family planning

Nowadays, whenever the subject of human love and marriage is discussed, family planning is soon mentioned. It is a widely held belief that one of the most serious problems to be solved by young people getting married, is that of preventing children arriving too soon or in too great a number. This attitude is altogether wrong. It is a kind of mental sickness in society which creates problems that ought never to have existed.

For every hundred who marry, probably ten will have difficulty in having children and many of them will never be able to achieve pregnancy. The latter group will certainly not have the problem of avoiding pregnancy, but should be encouraged by the fact that the Billings Ovulation Method of Natural Fertility Regulation is becoming the primary management of the problem of apparent infertility.

The peak of the couple's fertility is usually determined by the fertility of the woman. The peak of female fertility is usually between 20 and 25 years, with a gradual decline thereafter, the decline becoming much steeper after the age of 35. Once the age of 40 has been reached about 50 per cent of marriages have become sterile. There are some married couples whose fertility was high enough for conception in the first few years of married life, but who lost the opportunity of having children through postponing their effort to do so until the natural decline of fertility had brought it below a level at which conception was possible.

My own observations have persuaded me that the avoidance of pregnancy in the early years of married life, whatever the means adopted, imposes a serious strain upon the marriage. The marriage may survive it, or it may not.

If young people could be persuaded to marry with a willingness and eagerness to follow their natural inclinations in their love-making, and to leave to Almighty God the decision as to whether they will have children immediately or not, there would be many more stable and happy marriages in the community than there are at present. Family planning would be recognised as being only a temporary expedient for the majority, to be applied when sexual maturity and harmony in living together make its acceptance easy for both the husband and wife.

Occasionally some serious problem, usually of a medical nature, makes the avoidance of pregnancy very desirable or even imperative. My own experience embraces an unusually high proportion of instances where there was a serious obligation for the husband and wife to avoid pregnancy by whatever morally lawful means were available.

Improved knowledge

Many people still have the idea that the choice rests between methods which are morally lawful but unreliable and those which are morally unlawful but dependable. The fact is, that even when the Rhythm Method alone was available to Catholics, it was able to achieve results as good as the contraceptive techniques which were then in vogue. As the efficiency of artificial methods have improved, and the pill been developed, there has been a corresponding improvement in the techniques for defining the fertile days thus improving the efficiency of the natural methods.

I have often wondered why some people have this curious opinion, that what is morally good is unlikely to be efficient. I have thought that it may be a misinterpretation of a passage in scripture when Our Lord said that "The children of this world are more prudent after their own fashion than the children of light"[23] It has always been my experience that, even at a material level, behaviour which is morally good is that which is most likely to be profitable. Good morals are certainly good medicine.

An emotional state close to panic has been provoked in certain individuals by unwarranted fear about population pressures, and this prevents a critical assessment of the various methods of family planning. I am firmly of the opinion that in-so-far-as family planning is considered necessary, it can be successfully accomplished by methods of harmony with the authentic Catholic teaching. Many people fail to realise that this is so. Most of the agitation for the introduction of the Birth Control Programmes in the developing countries was initiated in the United States of America, and was soon taken up by other rich countries, particularly in Scandinavia and Europe. It is unfortunate that the citizens of the United States who have exhibited a level of generosity towards their less fortunate brethren without parallel in the world's history, should be obsessed with the idea that the under-developed nations must be persuaded to accept the contraceptive programmes which are offensive to so many, Christians and non-Christians alike. Malcolm Muggeridge, who was not at that time a Catholic, wisely condemned these "colporteurs of sterility who so complacently and self-righteously display their assortment of contraceptives to the so-called backward peoples of the world as our civilisation's noblest achievement and most precious gift."[24]

Truth and Love

In March 1995 Pope John Paul II published an Encyclical Letter *Evangelium Vitae* (The Gospel of Life) in which he emphasised the incomparable value of every human person, appealing to all humanity in the name of God to "respect, protect, love and serve life, every human life!" (n.5). He went on to write that "we are facing an enormous and dramatic clash between good and evil, death and life, the 'culture of death' and the 'culture of life'. We find ourselves not only faced with but necessarily in the midst of this conflict: we are all involved and we all share in it, with the inescapable responsibility of choosing to be unconditionally pro-life" (n.28).

In an earlier Encyclical *Veritatis Splendor* (The Splendour of Truth, 1993) John Paul II supported Paul VI

in defining contraception in *Humanae Vitae* as
intrinsically evil, pointing out that, "If acts are intrinsically
evil, good intention or particular circumstances can
diminish their evil, but they cannot remove it. They
remain 'irremediably' evil acts" (n.81).

A human being is entitled and indeed obliged to follow
a properly-formed conscience, that is, a conscience which
has been formed after careful and prayerful study. It is
possible for conscience to be in error for conscience does
not have a primary position in Catholic moral teaching:
primacy belongs to Truth and Love. A Catholic therefore
remembers Christ's promise to be with his Church and to
protect it from error until the end of time, and looks to the
teaching of the magisterium of the Church for guidance in
the formation of a correct conscience, knowing that if he
follows a correct conscience he will be in good conscience.

In *Veritatis Splendor* Pope John Paul II quotes, as he so
often does, the documents of the Second Vatican Council,
in this case the Pastoral Constitution of the Church in the
Modern World (*Gaudium et Spes*) which provides a
number of examples of acts which are intrinsically evil:
"Whatever is hostile to life itself, such as any kind of
homicide, genocide, abortion, euthanasia and voluntary
suicide; whatever violates the integrity of the human
person, such as mutilation, physical and mental tortures and
attempts to coerce the spirit; whatever is offensive to human
dignity, such as sub-human living conditions, arbitrary

imprisonment, deportation, slavery, prostitution and trafficking in women and children; degrading conditions of work which treat labourers as mere instruments of profit, and not as free responsible persons: all these and the like are a disgrace, and so long as they infect human civilization they contaminate those who inflict them more than those who suffer injustice, and they are a negation of the honour due to the Creator." (*Gaudium et Spes,* n.27)

The culture of death must be overcome by Truth and Love which can lead us to what both Pope Paul VI and Pope John Paul II refer to as "a Civilization of Love".

Artificial or natural

In forming an attitude of conscience towards moral problems it is important to understand the distinction between the purpose which it is intended to achieve and the means which are employed. No matter how much the situation demands a responsible decision by the husband and wife to avoid pregnancy, they are never at liberty to employ means which are intrinsically evil. There are many convincing reasons of a moral, philosophical, or psychological character why artificial methods are to be rejected. Here I shall refer only to the medical considerations.

Contraception means one of two things, thus:

1. A derangement of the act of sexual intercourse itself, for example by use of a condom, or diaphragm, or by incomplete intercourse (withdrawal or *coitus interruptus*).

2. The production of temporary or permanent suppression, or destruction of the fertility of either the husband or the wife, so that the normal act of sexual intercourse does not cause conception.

It is dishonest to describe procedures which involve destruction of the embryo as "contraception". Conception is accomplished as soon as the sperm enters the ovum and this is the beginning of a new human life.

When chemical contraception was introduced and it was understood that birth-control could be effected by the medication, a campaign was launched to persuade doctors to introduce an entirely new definition of pregnancy, that it does not begin until after implantation of the embryo. That is of course scientific nonsense and destruction of the embryo from the time of entry of the sperm into the ovum is abortion. It is to the discredit of the medical profession that such a large number of doctors followed the recommendation mentioned.

With natural methods of family planning the act of sexual intercourse is normal and there is no interference of any kind with a normal biological mechanism. The act of sexual intercourse always remains open to the transmission of life. It is for these reasons that more and more people are developing a preference for a natural method, coming to see later the wisdom of their choice. Catholic teaching on the subject of birth control is for the present a minority opinion in the world. It has not always been a minority opinion and the time will come when it is not a minority opinion any more.

AIDS

The disease AIDS (Acquired Immune Deficiency Syndrome) is due to a Retrovirus HIV-1 or the closely related Retrovirus HIV-2 and is a cause of very grave concern. It was recognized first in the United States of America in 1981 and was noted to have developed first as the result of anal intercourse amongst male homosexuals. By 1984 the virus was isolated and later the two closely related viruses were recognised. Gradually it was perceived that infection could be caused by the sharing of syringes and needles by intravenous drug-users, blood transfusion and even by breast milk. It was also soon clear that the virus could be transmitted from male to female or from female to male as the result of natural intercourse. In some cases the child in the womb has been infected by the presence of the disease in the mother.

An internationally orchestrated campaign to promote the use of condoms as an effective protection against the spread of AIDS and of other sexually-transmitted infections has followed. Many people wondered how a condom which was unable always to block the transmission of a sperm could be expected to block a tiny virus.

The educational programmes advocating the use of condoms as an effective defence against the transmission of AIDS has had catastrophic results. It has attracted into the dangerous lifestyle of sexual promiscuity involving many partners, or has caused many people already in that lifestyle to remain there, and that is why in the present state of medical science the terrible disease of AIDS continues to spread.

The isolation of the AIDS virus had been followed by the discovery that the virus in Africa was to be found amongst some monkeys and it is suspected that infection from these monkeys had initiated the human epidemic. There had been recognised in Africa a fatal human malady given the name of the "Thin Disease" because of the progressive cachexia (weakness and severe wasting) so characteristic of AIDS, and AIDS it was proved to be.

In the United States of America there is a group of Centers for Disease Control, linked with the main Center which is located in Atlanta, Georgia, U.S.A. In February 1987 a Conference entitled "Condoms in the Prevention of Sexually-Transmitted Diseases" was sponsored by the American Social Health Association, Family Health International and the Centers for Disease Control; the Conference was held in Atlanta.

The following quotation is taken from the summary issued after the Conference:

"Prevention through avoiding exposure is the best strategy for controlling the spread of Sexually-Transmitted Diseases (STDs). Behaviour that eliminates or reduces the risk of one

STD will likely reduce the risk of all STDs. Prevention of one case of STD can result in the prevention of many subsequent cases. Abstinence or sexual intercourse with one mutually faithful, uninfected partner are the only totally effective prevention strategies. Proper use of condoms with each act of sexual intercourse can reduce, but not eliminate risk of STD. Individuals likely to become infected or known to be infected with human immunodeficiency virus (HIV) should be aware that condom use cannot completely eliminate the risk of transmission to themselves or to others."[24a]

It is therefore the promotion of condoms and the resulting sexual promiscuity that must be charged with the causation of the continuing spread of HIV/AIDS throughout the world. It is a responsibility for parents, doctors, nurses, school teachers, Bishops and Priests to teach the only real effective way for a person to make sure of not acquiring the disease through sexual contact, and this can be taught as a simple rule of life: *Chastity Before Marriage, Fidelity in Marriage*. Clearly the marriage should be between two people who have followed this pattern (lifestyle) before marriage.

The Billings Ovulation Method exercises a therapy upon the marriage relationship and this is reported all over the world, amongst people of different cultures, different religions or no religion at all, and the method is particularly applicable when there exists some disturbance within the marriage such as selfishness, alcoholism and so on. One has had the experience of quite remarkable success in the restoration of happiness and security to the marriage by introducing the Billings Ovulation Method.

There have been reports from a number of African countries including Nigeria and Malawi that if teaching of the Billings Ovulation Method is established amongst the people, it enables them to reach the goal of commitment and security. There has been reported a highly significant difference between those couples living in a faithful marriage and using the Billings Ovulation Method, and those couples who have no knowledge of the method and in whom there is often infidelity which introduces the virus into the relationship.

In recent years there have been further studies of the use of condoms particularly with reference to AIDS, and the conclusions published in March 1988 have been confirmed.

These facts should be the core of teaching people about AIDS, as everyone is entitled to be told the truth. Everyone is able, especially with the help of God's grace, to change to a moral way of living from an immoral way, and is more likely to do so if the person giving information about the Billings Ovulation Method knows that this is possible.

The natural sequence

God in His infinite wisdom created women in such a fashion that during their reproductive years they are more often infertile than fertile. The person who believes in God will conclude that there must have been some very sound purpose in His mind. The complex sequence of events which determines the occurrence of ovulation is such that, even when the woman ovulates more than once in the menstrual cycles, these ovulations occur close together, usually within an hour; there is only *one ovulation day* in any cycle. Allowing for the continuing nourishment of the husband's cells within the wife's body, there are only about 7-8 days, and often less time, during each cycle, when conception is possible. It is part of the natural order of God's Creation that there are more days of infertility in the cycle than days of possible fertility, and so the couple is provided with considerable freedom for the expression of their conjugal love in sexual intercourse.

The fertile time

For the Catholic, the avoidance of pregnancy, if necessary, is achieved by the method of periodic continence, the avoidance of intercourse at those times when conception may follow. The success of the method depends on the accurate delineation of the infertile days. For many years the infertile days were predicted on the basis of the variations in the length of the menstrual cycles. This menstruation method or Rhythm Method, had the basic defect of all methods involving prediction, that the pattern on which the prediction was based might alter; in this instance, the menstrual cycles might suddenly change their length, and the prediction regarding infertile days would be incorrect. In addition, if allowance were made for considerable variation due to irregularity of the cycles, the days available for intercourse in each cycle became few in number.

Detecting ovulation

The day of ovulation in the menstrual cycle is located about 2 weeks before the following menstruation, and after ovulation the egg cell (*ovum*) lives less than 24 hours. If we can demonstrate that ovulation has occurred, we can at least be sure of about 10-12 days of infertility up to the menstrual period. This is accomplished in natural methods of fertility regulation such as the Ovulation Method, the Temperature Method, and temperature-based methods such as the Sympto-Thermal Methods. These methods therefore eliminate any difficulties or unreliability arising out of menstrual irregularity, and have disposed of the major problem of the Rhythm Method.

The contraceptive pill does not regulate ovulation and therefore cannot regulate the menstrual cycles. The pharmaceutical industries produced a dosage and a schedule of administration which provokes episodes of bleeding resembling menstrual bleeding and separated by an interval which is about the average length of the menstrual cycle. In other words it is a deception when the claim is made that this is "regulating the cycles". The truth is that the normal cycle has been abolished and manipulated bleeding has been substituted for it. Chemical contraception, whether by the Pill, implants or injections is an assault upon the reproductive physiology of the woman, and there are many complications which result, including a number which are of a very serious nature involving blood clotting, pulmonary embolism, strokes and heart attacks.

The Billings Ovulation Method, being a natural method, is completely harmless and it has an effectiveness in providing for the spacing of pregnancies that is not exceeded by any method of avoiding pregnancy, natural or otherwise. In addition, as has been noted above, it is able to provide substantial help to the couple having difficulty in achieving conception.

With competent teaching and adherence to the guidelines for the avoidance of pregnancy, trials of the Billings Ovulation Method in recent years have consistently shown a success rate of better than 99% and some have shown 100% success. There is no method of postponing pregnancy, natural or otherwise, that can do better than that and most methods cannot do as well. Such a result is obtained in the trial in China in 1998-9, a comparative trial where the effectiveness of the Billings Ovulation Method was shown to be markedly superior to that of the Intra-Uterine Device. In the Billings Ovulation Method group of 992 couples had no method-related pregnancy; there were 5 pregnancies which occurred as a result of an error made by couples who had not completed their instruction in the method. In the IUD group of 662 subjects, there were 12 pregnancies, while 38 women had to have the IUD removed on account of pain and haemorrhage and in another 15 cases the IUD was expelled from the uterus. It is to be remembered that additional pregnancies would have occurred in the IUD group but were not recognized, because the IUD destroys the embryo at implantation.[25a]

The following facts should be appreciated:

1. Irregularity of the menstrual cycles has ceased to be a problem in fertility regulation, and treatment to "regulate the cycles" is unnecessary.

2. In each menstrual cycle, there are more days of infertility than days on which conception is possible.

3. Every woman is able to be taught to recognise days of infertility in every cycle.

The problem which persisted longest in the refinement of natural techniques of fertility regulation was that of teaching the woman to recognise infertility prior to ovulation, in sufficient time to allow for the sperm survival. This problem has been solved by the most modern of natural methods, the "Ovulation Method," also now commonly called the "Billings Method".[25]

Observable signs

All women who are capable of bearing children, even if they are both uneducated and unintelligent, can learn to recognise certain symptoms which occur in their own bodies as an indication of fertility or infertility. The Billings Ovulation

Method is a completely new method which has had more scientific research devoted to it than any other method of regulating fertility, and that scientific research has validated all the guidelines of the method in its application for the achievement or the postponement of pregnancy.

The woman is able to recognise fertility by a vaginal discharge of mucus, which comes from the cervix (neck) of the uterus and is present usually for about 5-6 consecutive days, located approximately two weeks before menstruation. The woman would have been aware of this discharge ever since she became sexually mature, without perhaps every having learned to understand its meaning. Even when she may have a chronic vaginal discharge from infection, she can still be helped by a competent teacher to identify the changes which occur in that discharge when the cervical mucus indicating fertility is present. The important discharge begins a few days before ovulation and changes its characteristics from day to day, particularly changes in the sensation felt by the vulva outside the vagina. The mucus discharge is provoked by a rising level of oestrogens in the circulation as she approaches ovulation; on the day of ovulation or immediately before ovulation this discharge has a very lubricative character, producing a feeling of slipperiness on the vulva, this being the most useful and important sign of high fertility.[25b]

Every woman whose body is in a healthy state and who is capable of bearing children is familiar with the mucus symptom, although she may not previously have understood its significance. The cervical mucus is an essential fertility factor, so that in the Ovulation Method we are studying fertility itself. If the woman does not have satisfactory mucus, she will be unable to become pregnant, even though she ovulates and has intercourse with a fertile husband at that time.

The Ovulation Method is a technique of training the woman to understand her own cervical mucus pattern, so that she can define days of infertility, days of possible fertility and the days of maximum fertility in each menstrual cycle. It is very desirable that young women should learn to understand their own physiological processes, especially the physiology of the reproductive system. With this knowledge, which the woman can easily communicate to her husband, the husband and wife have an option available to them, to engage in coitus during the fertile days of the cycle if it is their intention to achieve pregnancy, and to refrain from all genital contact during the fertile days of the cycle if it is their intention to avoid pregnancy.

Additionally, the knowledge may help the couple to overcome the problem of infertility. There are some women in whom a satisfactory mucus secretion occurs only occasionally, perhaps only for one day or part of one day in the particular cycle. If the woman is aware of the significance of the lubricative, slippery mucus which indicates a high state of fertility, she and her husband can ensure that intercourse occurs at that time.

The Ovulation Method has found great applicability in the developing countries of the world because it gives to the husband and wife complete freedom to use the method just as they wish. However, it is also particularly useful in the affluent societies, as it brings husband and wife into confrontation with their fertility in each cycle, an occurrence which has a profound effect upon their relationship and attitude to life. It helps to put the child back at the centre of concern and love within the family.

Because the Ovulation Method enables the woman to identify the presence of infertility even if ovulation is delayed, it is applicable during breast-feeding, and through the years leading to menopause, situations which the other natural methods are incapable of handling. The Peak symptom as defined in the Ovulation Method is the most dependable of all the natural biological markers of the time of ovulation, and therefore does not require to be "checked" by any other marker, such as the less precise temperature indication. The Ovulation Method is a method to be used alone as the inaccuracies of the Temperature Method can create confusion. This is because the Temperature Method is a non-specific method, meaning that the temperature can be disturbed by influences which have nothing to do with the woman's reproductive system. Furthermore the Temperature Method is sometimes inaccurate, which can cause confusion and discouragement because the indications provided by the two methods will be in contradiction.

If knowledge of the Ovulation Method were universal, the tragedy of premarital pregnancies would in many cases be avoided. As the young girl approaches sexual maturity the mother should inform her about menstruation and also about the possibility of a vaginal discharge which is the healthy cervical mucus. Ideally this information should be provided and continued through adolescence, and it is very desirable that the teacher is the mother. The adolescent girl is becoming a woman, meaning that this is the time that psychological maturity is achieved, to match her physical maturity. The cervical mucus is explained as an indication that the girl is developing towards a stage when she will be able to become a mother. This exchange of information helps to establish a level of solidarity between the mother and the daughter, at the time when some degree of estrangement may occur. The girl now becomes interested in her fertility and appreciative of the wonderful gift that the Creator has given her, so she begins to think about the possibility of babies in the future and determines to protect the fertility from any possibility of harm.

Maturity and understanding

There are some people who consider that the observation of the natural workings of the body is somehow improper, or at least indelicate. These people often regard certain parts of their bodies as "rude" or "obscene." This indicates an unhealthy attitude about sexual matters in general, with conscious or repressed feelings of guilt on the subject.

Observation of natural phenomena is a study of God's creation and the Catholic attitude is one of co-operation with God in the protection and proper use of what He has provided. The observations do not lead to hypochondriasis, for the hypochondriac mistakes natural occurrences for the expression of disease. In learning more about the workings of her body, the woman learns that symptoms she may previously have observed but not understood, can now be recognised as an indication of normal health.

It is sometimes said that periodic abstinence is likely to create emotional difficulties between the husband and wife. This may be so in the first few years of marriage, and more particularly when the reasons for the avoidance of pregnancy are trivial, so that the husband and wife may then disagree on the need for abstinence and one regard the attitude of the other as an indication of lack of affection. It may be difficult to secure the co-operation of the husband or wife if they have not been properly instructed in the method and assured of its effectiveness. Despite the reliability and easy application of modern natural methods of the regulation of births, unfortunately there is evidence that couples, already anxious about the risks attached to a further pregnancy, have been upset by incorrect statements from people with vested interests, which deny the excellent results of the Billings Ovulation Method.

The demand for the right to engage in sexual intercourse at any time that the inclination exists can be an expression of a sexual immaturity for which the only cure is periodic continence; unchecked, it may destroy the very love it purports to express and to foster.

My own experience includes a number of instances of complaints that the excessive demands of the husband made the avoidance of intercourse on days of possible fertility impossible. This situation has commonly arisen from emotional frustration on the part of the husband, arising out of the wife's poor responsiveness to his loving advances. A vicious circle is easily set up, so that the more intemperate the demands, the chillier the reception. If the wife will give her husband a loving welcome during the days of infertility, co-operating warmly in the act of love, the problem will often disappear.

A deepening mental harmony

It has been my experience that periodic continence may have a very beneficial effect upon the psychological relationship of the husband and wife to one another. The physical embrace of conjugal love is frequently refreshed by rest, and it is very important for married persons to learn that love is expressed in many other ways. Sometimes it does create difficulty and the wise husband or wife who perceives this learns a new measure of the other's love. There are words sometimes used in marriage services which put it this way, "Sacrifice is usually difficult and irksome. Only love can make it a joy. We are willing to give in proportion as we love. And when love is perfect the sacrifice is complete."[26] And there is no remedy save love for the fear of the woman who believes, rightly or wrongly, that her life will be imperilled by further pregnancy; "Love drives out fear."[27]

Periodic continence may also assist those persons whose inclination to lovemaking depends upon physical rather than mental stimuli, although the argument is sometimes expressed the other way about. One hears objection at times to the use of the method of periodic continence because there may be maximal inclination for intercourse in the woman on the days of maximal fertility. Careful observations of large numbers of women have demonstrated that there is no consistent relationship between the inclination for intercourse and fertility. It is helpful however to point out that the time of maximal fertility can be recognised by the woman in the observation of a wetness and slippery feeling on the vulva. This is very useful for those couples who have had difficulty in achieving pregnancy but who have a strong desire for a child of their own.

Later on in married life, however, sexual intercourse finds its true place as an expression of a deepening mental harmony and unity between the husband and wife. When love reaches this maturity it is the spiritual unity which determines the inclination for physical unity, at the times of greatest joy and love in their life together.

The absurdity of the thesis that a woman has inclination for sexual intercourse only during days of fertility becomes evident when one considers the physiology of lactation. While she is fully breast-feeding her child, a woman most often experiences suspension of ovulation for several months, perhaps a year or more. It is totally absurd to suggest that during all of that time she will feel no inclination for intercourse.

Natural methods

When used to avoid pregnancy, the natural methods of family planning involve complete abstinence from genital contact during the days of possible fertility. When the fertile phase is over, some women feel that they have lost inclination for intercourse. It is helpful to explain that she now has the opportunity to return the generous love her husband has given in his self-restraint for her good and the good of the family, by making a positive conscious effort to be attractive and to invite her husband to the physical act of love. The woman who loves her husband readily understands that he will respond immediately to this loving invitation. She will find great joy in his responsiveness and in her ability to satisfy all his physical and emotional needs. The infertile time is then awaited with joyful anticipation by both husband and wife, and their great awareness of each other can even enable them to experience a level of happiness hitherto unknown in their marriage. The application of the natural methods has promoted the development of greater communication and co-operation between them, virtues which are essential to the stability of marriage itself.

Responsibility for parenthood

Cardinal Karol Wojtyla, later to become Pope John Paul II, said: "Responsibility for parenthood is engendered through conjugal love, understood and experienced in a responsible way, that is, according to all its interior truth, in the fullness of the sense and meaning of love. Thus understood and experienced, responsibility for parenthood allows the husband and wife to pose the problem of responsible parenthood correctly in their thinking, their appraisal and their judgement, and also to solve that problem correctly in their life and concrete behaviour. If this correctness reaches the sphere of the so-called methods of birth control, even here the husband and wife will not forego what constitutes the authentic measure of responsibility of love, and therefore both the essential value of the person, and the dignity of parenthood connected with it. Speaking more plainly: they will not have recourse to contraception, which is essentially opposed to love and parenthood."[27a]

Respecting God's creative intent

The Constitution 'Gaudium et Spes' of the Second Vatican Council told us: "married people should realise that in their behaviour they may not simply follow their own fancy but must be ruled by conscience - and conscience ought to be conformed to the law of God in the light of the teaching authority of the Church, which is the authentic interpreter of Divine Law". (n.50)

Most of us have sufficient familiarity with domestic or farm animals to know that the female animal has a sexual season and this is the only time that she will receive the male. The human female also has a limited time of fertility, such that on the majority of days in her reproductive cycle it is impossible for her to become pregnant. However, it is a particularly human phenomenon that the conjugal embrace occurs throughout the cycle, and is not restricted to the time of fertility. The physical union now exercises a power additional to the achievement of pregnancy. It is unitive as well as procreative, giving intermittent expression to what should be a permanent state of psychological and spiritual union between the spouses and has its origin in the commitment that their total, exclusive love for each other has inspired them to make.

Human fertility is a wonderful gift, enabling the husband and wife to share by an act of love in the creation of a new human life: a new, unique human being to live in God's family for eternity. This fertility is of primary importance in the gift which the husband and wife give to the other and accept from the other when they declare that henceforth there will not be two lives but one life in common. The realisation of this truth motivates them to respect and protect their fertility, to understand and practise responsible parenthood.

It is not difficult to understand that the Creator, by providing days of infertility both before and after the fertile days, has provided for those circumstances when the couple, faced with medical, economic or other problems, should prudently postpone pregnancy, at least for the time being. Without suppressing or destroying their fertility, without distorting the marital act of love, they can continue to express and foster their love, in happiness with each other and with their children. The woman's reproductive cycle is a manifestation of God's creative intent at any particular time. During the days of pre-ovulatory and post-ovulatory infertility it is God's will that intercourse will not result in pregnancy, whereas during the fertile phase it is God's creative will that an act of intercourse can result in pregnancy. When there is a need to postpone pregnancy the spouses find other ways to express their love during the fertile phase, not least by the sacrifice involved in the acceptance of abstinence from genital contact for the sake of the beloved person. There is total acceptance of God's will as it is demonstrated in human biology.

BENEFITS AND CHALLENGES

Now that it is becoming common knowledge that the modern methods of natural family planning have a level of effectiveness in the postponement of pregnancy which is not exceeded by any contraceptive or sterilising technique, there has developed a deeper insight into the beneficial effects of the use of a natural method upon the conjugal relationship. A better level of communication is achieved: deeper insight into each other's physical and emotional needs. The couple learns to look at their combined fertility and decide together what they will do: there is a sharing of responsibility in the achievement of the intended result. Most of all there is a demonstration of a willingness to accept the gentle discipline required so that self-respect and love grow as both husband and wife observe in themselves and each other the goodness of which they are capable. Every human life becomes precious, especially the lives which may be the product of their love, and the child is restored to its rightful place at the centre of concern within the family.

As Pope John Paul II said in '*Familiaris Consortio*': "The choice of the natural rhythms involves accepting the cycle of the person, that is the woman, and thereby accepting dialogue, reciprocal respect, shared responsibility and self-control. To accept the cycle and to enter into dialogue means to recognise both the spiritual and corporal character of conjugal communion, and to live personal love with its requirement of fidelity. In this context the couple comes to experience how conjugal communion is enriched with those values of tenderness and affection which constitute the inner soul of human sexuality, in its physical dimension also". (n.32)

Familiaris Consortio was published as a result of the work of the 1980 Synod of Bishops in Rome on the theme of "The Role of the Christian Family in the Modern World", in which my wife Lyn and I had the privilege of participating as auditors. The Synod referred to the Encyclical *Humanae Vitae* of Pope Paul VI and fully reconfirmed its teaching.

Pope Paul VI taught us in *Humanae Vitae* that the discipline of natural family planning "bestows upon family life fruits of serenity and peace, and facilitates the solution of other problems; it favours attention for one's partner, helps both parties to drive out selfishness, the enemy of true love; and deepens their sense of responsibility". (n21)

Facing difficulties

On 5th June 1987, at the Vatican, Pope John Paul II received in audience the participants in a Study Conference on responsible procreation, sponsored by the Centre for Studies and Research on the Natural Regulation of Fertility of the Department of Medicine of the Catholic

University of the Sacred Heart in Rome, at which I was present. In the course of his address, the Holy Father said:

"Notwithstanding the difficulties you may encounter, it is necessary to continue with generous dedication.

The difficulties you encounter are of various kinds. The first, and in a certain sense the most serious, is that even within the Christian community voices have been heard, and are still being heard, which cast doubt upon the very truth of the Church's teaching. This teaching has been vigorously expressed by Vatican II, by the Encyclical *'Humanae Vitae'*, by the Apostolic Exhortation *'Familiaris Consortio'* and by the recent Instruction *'The Gift of Life'*. A grave responsibility derives from this: those who place themselves in open conflict with the law of God, authentically taught by the Church, guide spouses along a false path. The Church's teaching on contraception does not belong to the category of matter open to free discussion among theologians. Teaching the contrary amounts to leading the moral consciences of spouses into error.

The second difficulty is constituted by the fact that many think that the Christian teaching, though true, is yet impracticable, at least in some circumstances. As the Tradition of the Church has constantly taught, God does not command the impossible, but every Commandment also carries with it a gift of Grace which assists human freedom in fulfilling it. However, there is need for constant prayer, frequent recourse to the Sacraments and the exercise of conjugal chastity".

Something in combined opinion

There may be individuals, even amongst the clergy, who are
deceived by the protestations of some married couples
regarding the difficulties of periodic continence. As
Newman said with regard to matters of doctrine, "There is
something in the combined opinion of the pastors and the
laity (*pastorum et fidelium conspiratio*) which is not in the
pastors alone"[28]. The pastors can be assured that a very large
body of lay opinion in the Church can perceive, with
greater or less clarity as the case may be, the fundamental
wisdom and goodness of the teaching of the Church
regarding contraception. This body of opinion was not
moulded by the traditional teaching so much as having
resulted from personal experience of the application of the
teaching, which might in the first instance have been
regarded as irksome. There is much to be written and
understood yet regarding the theology of periodic
continence, but I am sure that there are many happy
marriages which would not have survived if there had not
been times of continence when there was a strong inclination
for intercourse. Love must be generous, and must serve the
good of the person loved and the good of the family.
Malcolm Muggeridge grasped a good deal of the distinction
between love and sex when he wrote, "Sex begins in passion
which comprehends the concepts of both suffering and joy;
it ends in a trivial dream of pleasure which itself soon
dissolves into the solitude and despair of self-gratification"[29].

Principle under challenge

It is a common tactic for a moral principle to be challenged by the presentation of a "hard case". This tactic has been used to promote legislation to allow for induced abortion, at first for specified situations such as: a serious threat to the life of the mother resulting from the pregnancy; if the child is conceived as a result of rape; if the pregnant woman is threatening to commit suicide if she has to carry the child to term; and where the ante-natal examinations have indicated the presence of some abnormality in the child. It is necessary to understand that no woman really wants to kill her child but she may need compassionate and effective help to solve the problem that has resulted from the pregnancy.

When a life-threatening situation develops during pregnancy, the doctor has to remember that he has two patients in his care. He must not kill the mother to save the child, nor kill the child to save the mother. He must strive to save the two lives. There are many examples of women who have refused abortion for a pregnancy caused by rape, and they tell wonderfully happy stories of the effect it has on the child when at an appropriate age the facts regarding her conception are revealed to her; this results in a great intensity of the love the children develop towards their mother. Statistics show that psychiatrists as a group have a higher incidence of suicide than do pregnant women. In recent years there has been much angry criticism from those with congenital physical or intellectual disorders when they hear of proposals for legislation which would prove that they have no right to be alive at all.

In short, one can say that good morals make good medicine and that there is never a reason that can justify the horrendous crime of abortion.

It is generally appreciated that women have a great longing to be loved. It should be equally evident that men too also have a great longing to be loved, and that the person a married man most wants to love him, is his wife. Many problems in marriage develop first with the wife becoming afraid of a further pregnancy, which may make her unresponsive to her husband's requests for intercourse developing to the point when intercourse occurs very infrequently, if at all. The husband often shares the desire to postpone a further pregnancy and will sometimes begin to take a lot of alcohol with the hope that this may reduce his requests or even angry demands for intercourse, whereas it often has the opposite effect of reducing his self-control, so that he may have outbursts of anger or become physically abusive. If in those circumstances the woman seeks a solution in surgical sterilisation, the situation deteriorates markedly, as the husband now believes that she has no reason at all to refuse intercourse, as she is "no longer a complete woman", an opinion she may have already begun to form about herself.

Fifty years of experience in the application of a reliable natural family planning method have demonstrated that the Billings Method can very often solve these problems. The woman can quickly understand the basic principles of the method and know that she can confidently be sure of all the days of infertility in the cycle. She can then be encouraged to make use of those days in such a way to demonstrate to her husband that she does really love him. The situation may have deteriorated to a point when she can find this very difficult at first, but she can be promised that if she makes the effort then one day her husband will repay her with his love and care.

Counselling

Priests, doctors and others are often approached for counsel regarding problems of married life including family planning. They know well enough, but cannot be reminded too often of the fact, that when people seek advice, there is a presenting problem, and in most cases a far more important and significant basic problem. Furthermore, each may be both a moral problem and an emotional problem. The latter is of very considerable importance. Until they have been emotionally stabilised by an understanding priest who accepts them as individual persons of great value, few people will be able to accept his moral direction; this is true even though Catholic people naturally look to the priest to obtain certainty of conscience. For a person to accept the fact that approval of a particular course of action cannot be obtained, and to move to the positive action of seeking instruction so that he can apply himself to a moral solution of the problem, much time must be expended in the counselling. It requires also that a priest must be able to judge whether a particular recommendation, for example, regarding medical treatment, is likely to be morally lawful or not. If he lacks the necessary medical knowledge, he has an obligation to seek advice about it. He needs to know that modern methods of natural family planning do not require regularity of the menstrual cycles, and that there is no scientific evidence at all that the pill will regulate the cycles.

The art of counselling

The correct definition of counsel is that it is advice, opinion or instruction given in order to direct another person in the judgement of his conduct. People who ask for counsel in regard to matters of morality have come to be helped to understand and to do what is right, that is, what is for their ultimate good.

When an individual comes to a spiritual counsellor for guidance in the formation of his conscience, he does not want to be told, "Just follow your conscience", he wants to know what his conscience ought to be telling him. He is seeking not merely to be in good conscience, but also to know how to be in right conscience. It is foolish and a betrayal of his trust, to say, "If you believe that in your circumstances it is right to do such and such an action, then do it". What is good is not a matter of merely human opinion; the summons to do good does not present alternatives, it imposes a duty. There are certain actions which a human person ought to do, and others that he ought not to do. Charity demands that we help people to do what they ought and not to do things which they ought not to do. The God in whom we believe is a God of love, and to help people to act in obedience to His laws is to work in the service of love. So the expression "non-directive counselling" is an absurdity, except in-so-far-as the counsellor helps the client to make his own firm decision to act correctly. It is psychotherapy for neurosis that requires to be non-directive, not spiritual counselling.

Facing the real problem

It is only with considerable experience that one recognises how often the client avoids discussion of the real problem, especially in the early sessions, even when he has sought the consultation voluntarily. He must be encouraged to talk about himself, whilst the counsellor pays attention and loves him. This love is not purely intellectual but needs also to be felt emotionally. Reassurance should be used sparingly at first, as a client is well aware that the basic problem cannot yet be understood. The ultimate aim is that he should understand his own problem adequately, and decide on a course of action for himself. If it becomes clear that the man is not only withdrawing from contact with his family, but also from his club, his sporting activities and his hobbies, the problem is not so much likely to be one to do with the marriage but with the man himself. If he is making excessive demands for intercourse, it may be that he is something of an effeminate individual, needing to demonstrate his manliness to himself. What is he trying to prove? is it that he feels uncertain of his wife's love and needs her acquiescence to reassure him? Perhaps he is an anxious individual, striving to allay his fears but using intercourse to help him sleep, or as a tranquiliser.

There are many situations in which complete acceptance of the client's moral attitudes may not be possible but he can always be accepted with friendliness and interest. It is well to bear in mind that all people are to some extent lonely, and also that many people are most truculent and argumentative when they are most uncertain of themselves.

Unhappiness and bitterness arising in marriage will reflect a sense of being unloved, and so often this is the product of misunderstanding or foolish thoughtlessness. The pain and anger would not occur if there were not love underneath; both parties need generosity and humility, a readiness to accept the weaknesses of the other and to acknowledge their own, for this is the way to happiness and peace. Their marriage has made them one in God's sight, each dependent upon the other. As St Paul told us, "If you are a wife, it may be your part to save your husband, for all you know; if a husband, for all you know, it may be your part to save your wife".[30]

Fear of too many children

For the majority of persons in normal health, living in reasonable economic circumstances, it would not be unreasonable to suggest that on getting married they should look forward to a family of 4 or 5 children. It they would do so, instead of allowing their married life to be plagued by the fear of too many children, it is certain that there would be fewer unhappy marriages, fewer divorces and that a large number of couples would discover that their fertility is surprisingly less than they had anticipated. What is also important, those who eventually found the avoidance of pregnancy necessary would have reached a state of sexual maturity and emotional harmony which permits them to take the problem in their stride.

The benefits of children are sometimes forgotten. For example, it should not be assumed that because a woman has a selfish or irresponsible husband that she should avoid pregnancy. If the husband cannot be assisted to more maturity and unselfishness in his conduct, it is likely that the marriage will disintegrate and the woman be abandoned and alone, perhaps in early middle life. At such a time, the children give her life much more purpose than it would have otherwise, as well as a good measure of happiness and companionship.

Overconcern

The tendency to be too concerned about the regulation of births brings its own problems. There are a number of married couples who in the past have tried to use natural techniques such as the Rhythm Method from the time they were first married. Either through inaccurate knowledge of the method or poor attention to the rules to be followed if it were the intention to avoid pregnancy, a number of pregnancies occurred. Eventually they acquired a moderate or even a large family, although throughout their married life they had more or less been trying to avoid pregnancy. Little wonder that they should complain of irritation and frustration regarding the physical expression of their love. How much better it would have been, and how much wiser, if they had allowed their natural inclinations to find normal expression, until the size of the family had made family planning seem wise. They have never known the joy of planning a baby, to be able to remember for the rest of their lives the love and joy that went into the creation of the child whom they see before them.

Contraception and abortion

Fear of the child and enmity towards the child have reached such a high level in the world today that the prevention of births has become an obsession for many people, so much so that they are indifferent as to whether this is effected by the prevention of conception or destruction of a new human life. Many modern techniques of "contraception" depend to some extent or even totally upon the destruction of the new human person who comes into existence at the moment of conception. Euphemistic terms are used to mask the truth. Methods have been devised to make the woman's body antagonistic to her husband's sperm cells, so that they will be rendered incapable of fertilising the ovum (contraception). Another technique is to immunise the women against the hormone produced by the human embryo within about a week of conception in order to protect his/her own life; the effect of this immunisation is to destroy the embryo (abortion). It does not require much imagination to recognise the danger of such misuse of medical knowledge. Bad morals make bad medicine.

A new abortion pill is now being used in many countries, mifepristone (RU486). The late Professor Jerome Lejeune, a famous geneticist appropriately dubbed RU486 as "the first human pesticide".

At the present time there are two methods of birth-control which are widely used:

1. Chemical methods, including the pill, implants and injections.

2. The intra-uterine device.

The intra-uterine device interferes with the implantation of the new life in the wall of the womb, so that deprived of maternal nourishment it dies. Some people try to distinguish the seriousness of this prevention of nidation (nesting) from the ejection of the new life after implantation, reserving the term abortion for the latter.

However, the distinction is really a deception: both processes involve the destruction of human life. Experts who use this method admit a failure rate of up to 5%[31]

The combined pill has three actions:

1. It tends to suppress ovulation. This is sterilisation. It involves a good deal more than a purely gynaecological effect.

2. It damages the cervix, preventing it from forming the healthy mucus secretion necessary to nourish the sperm cells and assist conception. This is a contraceptive action, as the sperm cells have been denied the help of the normal mucus necessary for them to reach the ovum.

3. It disturbs the regular preparation of the womb in each cycle for the reception of the embryo, the new life which may result if neither ovulation nor conception has been prevented. The lining membrane of the womb (endometrium) is then likely to reject the embryo. Thus the pill has an abortifacient action which is sometimes responsible for the prevention of a birth.

Most women bleed at monthly intervals, in an amount which approximates to that of the menstrual period, when they take the birth control pill according to the dosage and routine prescribed. It is unnecessary for them to follow this method of administration to avoid pregnancy, but it has the advantage for the pharmaceutical industries of concealing from the woman that her endocrine physiology is suffering a violent assault. The ordinary birth-control pill is a combination of an oestrogen and a gestogen, meaning chemicals which may be obtained from plants or manufactured in a laboratory, which simulate some but not all the function of natural oestrogens and the natural hormone progesterone. It is very important not to call the gestogens "progesterone" as they are not progesterone at all. These chemicals suppress the function of the hypothalamus (part of the brain), the pituitary gland and the ovaries, and this is a very serious disturbance, such that one can say quite positively that the action of chemical contraception is contrary to sound medical principles.

Suppression of natural function

There were many people who were opposed to the birth control pill on medical grounds from the time it was first used. They held the opinion that the suppression of a natural function of the body, such as ovulation, will inevitably produce harm. One would hold the same opinion if the function suppressed were, for example, unrelated to sexuality, such as the secretion of digestive juices. The complexities of the intracellular organs, make it inevitable that a serious derangement of any biological system will have repercussions throughout the whole body. This can be understood as a matter of common sense.

The time is now at hand when no women in her right mind will take birth control medication, no husband in his right mind will allow his wife to take it, and no doctor in his right mind will prescribe it. The idea of a "perfect pill" is an illusion. No problem on earth will be solved satisfactorily by the prolonged administration of drugs to healthy people. One should learn about natural processes in order to co-operate with them, not to derange or destroy them.

As we are told in Ecclesiastes, "There is a season for everything, a time for embracing, a time to refrain from embracing."[32] St Paul may have had these words in mind when he said, "Do not refuse each other except by mutual consent, and then only for an agreed time, to leave yourself free for prayer."[33]

Consequences of using the pill

Some women find that they do not bleed regularly when taking the pill. Whether they do or not, they tend to persist in their previous menstrual pattern when the periods become re-established after they have stopped taking the pill. In some cases the cycle pattern is disturbed so that the cycles are no longer regular, or are more irregular than they were previously. Occasionally protracted sterility requires special treatment and may indeed be incurable if the cervix (neck) of the womb has been damaged so that the normal mucus secretion does not return.

It is extraordinary how many serious complications have occurred as a result of the use of chemical contraception, however it is administered. Damage to the reproductive system was obvious but it was not predicted that blood clotting would commonly occur, caused both by the oestrogen and gestogen components. These can cause clotting in veins, pulmonary embolism caused by the blood clot progressing in the circulation to the lungs and blocking the blood supply to the lungs. The clots can also occur in the coronary arteries, producing heart attacks, or in the cerebral arteries causing strokes. High blood pressure is provoked in many cases, any tendency to diabetes is increased, severe depression and loss of libido are common, and there is an increased incidence of cancer of the breast and cancer of the ovaries. Prolonged and even permanent sterility is well documented.

The new "Abortion Pill" RU486 mentioned above acts by blocking the progesterone receptors in the woman's body, which is equivalent to eliminating the good effects of the rise of progesterone which occurs after ovulation in the normal cycle and continues to increase if pregnancy occurs. The word progesterone means "for the pregnancy". When the physiological influence of the progesterone is blocked, the woman's body will not maintain the pregnancy, so that induced abortion is a result. The drug is dangerous particularly in its provocation of very severe bleeding accompanying the abortion. In some countries RU486 is used repeatedly as a "Morning-after Pill" and there is as yet no real knowledge of what other serious dangers could appear when repeated treatment with RU486 may go on for years.

When it is remembered that all the complications of chemical contraception by pills, implants or injections can be avoided by a harmless natural method of regulating fertility, which acts with an effectiveness which is not exceeded by any other method at all, the use of any but the natural method will be recognised as a very foolish decision.

The difficulties, complications, dangers and failure rate of artificial methods of family planning are now more generally acknowledged. It is also becoming a matter of general knowledge that the modern methods of fertility regulation such as the Ovulation Method are simple, harmless and as reliable as any method of contraception or sterilisation. The truth is that continuing opposition to methods of regulating births which do not conflict with traditional Catholic teaching depends to a large extent for its vehemence upon an unwillingness to accept any restriction of the time available for coitus, upon resistance to the authority of the Church in matters of morality, or to the profit motive. The contraception-sterilisation-abortion package is a multi-national, multi-million dollar industry, whereas natural family planning is free.

The challenge

Our beloved Pope John XXIII expressed his wishes about the spirit he wished to permeate during his pontificate by quoting words from St John Chrysostom, "It would scarcely be necessary to expound Doctrine if our life were radiant enough; it would not be necessary to use words if our acts were witness enough. If we behaved like true Christians there would be no pagans".[34]

Francois Mauriac wrote these beautiful words:

"Christ will give you a clear understanding of what you are; an immortal soul, not one living in isolation, but one surrounded by a great many other souls over whom you exercise power for better or for worse.

When grace diminishes in you, it diminishes in a great many others who depend upon you. If you are a friend of Christ, many others will warm themselves at this fire, will share in this light.

The darkness of sin in you will cast its shadow over those whom you now enlighten. And the day when you no longer burn with love, many others will die of the cold."

One of the challenges to all Christians in their imitation of Christ is that of permeating the world with the Christian idea of sexual love, inspired by the faith and purity of the Virgin Mary, Mother of the Church, and her protector St Joseph. Individual chastity is the essential action - continence for the unmarried, selfless generosity of the celibate, and for the married generosity towards God and toward each other, for their love has not two aspects but one. None of us know what difficulties and suffering may, in God's providence, befall us. God wills our holiness in our present situation. We know that God is a God of Love, and that in some way His laws do service in the cause of love. We are living in a vale of tears, in a world where sickness, accidents, poverty, dissensions and hatred exist, as well as problems concerned with sexual loving. Faith is needed at times to see that strengthening the will to observe God's laws in the face of difficulty leads ultimately to the greatest good of the individual and of all people. Ronald Knox tells the story of 3 individual ways to Calvary. The impenitent thief is bitter and resentful. The penitent thief makes the best of it, acknowledging his faults and accepting his due of suffering. Christ Our Lord, wholly innocent, accepts the cross, His heart overflowing with love.[35] For here is the extraordinary fact to animate us as Christians, that the suffering of the innocent may be joined to Christ's redemptive suffering on Calvary and so help to effect the salvation of mankind.

APPENDIX

The Catechism of the Catholic Church

A glance at the index of the Catechism under the headings: *'Matrimony'*, *'Family'*, *'Parents; Children: Childrearing'*, gives an instant reference to the riches and wisdom to be found in this magnificent text which Pope John Paul II referred to as "...a sure norm for teaching the faith..." when he presented the Catechism and ordered its publication.

Note: Those numbers in the index printed in italics are cross-references and indicate relevant parallel passages.

Summary of the Catechism of the
Catholic Church References

The paragraphs and subjects listed in the above index are to be found in the Catechism under the following sections:

THE SACRAMENT OF MATRIMONY - Paragraphs 1601 - 1666 (pages 358 -372)*

THE FOURTH COMMANDMENT - Paragraphs 2197 - 2257 (pages 474 - 486)*

THE SIXTH COMMANDMENT - Paragraphs 2331 - 2400 (Pages 499 - 513)*
(*Refers to Geoffrey Chapman Edition.)

Notes

1. Pope Paul VI, *Humanae Vitae* n.21.
2. Karol Wojtyla, *"Fruitful and Responsible Love"*, Geoffrey Chapman, Australia.
3. Ronald Knox, *"Bridegroom and Bride"*, Sheed and Ward, London.
4. Pope John Paul II, *Address to the Pontifical Academy of Sciences,* 10 Nov. 1979.
5. St Thomas Aquinas. 1, 2, Q. 26 A. 4.
6. 1 John 4:8.
7. 1 John 4:12.
8. Antiphon for Maundy Thursday.
9. Pope Paul VI, *Letter to Bishops' Conference*, February 2, 1969.
10. Pope Paul VI, *Address during Holy Mass*, St Peter's, Rome, March 19, 1969.
11. Pope Paul VI, *Humanae Vitae*, N. 8 & 9.
12. Ephesians 5:23.
13. Ephesians 5:27.
14. Hugh of St Victor (1096-1141).
15. *"Germinal"* by A. E. Quoted by Graham Greene in *"The Lost Childhood and Other Essays"*, A Penguin Book, p.l6.

16. Tobias, 6:17.

16a. *Guide for Living: Selected Addresses and Letters of His Holiness Pope Pius XII*. Pan Books Ltd: London 1958. Part 1, The Family: 1: Conjugal Relations p.29.

17. Reginald Garrigou-Lagrange, O.P, *"Providence"*. B. Herder Book Company, St Louis, Mo., U.S.A.

18. Statement by Cardinal Suhard.

19. *"Natural Law Morality Today"* by Cahal B. Daly, Clonmore and Reynolds Ltd., Dublin.

20. *"Marriage and the Family"* from *"Society and Sanity"* by F. J. Sheed, Sheed and Ward, London.

21. Maccabees 2:1, 4.

22. Pope Paul VI, *Humanae Vitae*, n.25.

23. Luke 10:8.

24. Malcolm Muggeridge, *"What I Believe,"* Allan and Unwin, London.

24a. *Morbidity and Mortality Weekly Report*, Printed and distributed by the Massachusetts Medical Society: 11 March 1998/Vol. 37/No. 9.

25. *"'The Ovulation Method"*, *"Atlas of the Ovulation Method"'*, *"The Billings Method"*. Family Life Centre, 27 Alexander Pde, North Fitzroy, Victoria 3068, Australia.

25a. *Evaluation of the Effectiveness of a Natural Fertility Regulation Programme in China* by Shao-Zhen QIAN et alii. Bulletin of the Ovulation Method Research and Reference Centre of Australia 27, No. 4: 17-22, 2000.

25b. *The Billings Method* by Evelyn L Billings and Ann Westmore, Anne O'Donovan, Melbourne 2000. Distributed in the United Kingdom by Gracewing Publishers, London

26. The Marriage Service in the Baltimore Ritual.

27. 1 John 4:18.

27a. Karol Wojtyla, *"Fruitful and Responsible Love"*, Geoffrey Chapman, Australia.

28. J. H. Newman, *"On Consulting the Faithful in Matters of Doctrine"*, p.104. Published by Geoffrey Chapman, London.

29. Malcolm Muggeridge, *"Tread Softly for you Tread on my Jokes"*, Collins, London, p.56.

30. 1 Corinthians 7:16.
31. *Current trends in Population Control*. Nicholas J. Eastman, A. Ford Foundation reprint from "*Fertility and Sterility*", 1964 15,5.
32. Ecclesiastes 3:1, 8.
33. I Corinthians 7:5.
34. "*The Heart and Mind of John XXIII*" by Loris Capovilla, A Corgi Book, Transworld Publishers Ltd., London.
35. Ronald Knox, "*The Way of Love*", in "*A Retreat for Lay People*", Sheed and Ward, London.

Contacts for further information about the Ovulation Method (Billings)

Australia: The Ovulation Method Research and Reference Centre of Australia, 27 Alexandra Parade, North Fitzroy, Victoria, 3068, Australia. Tel: +61 3 9481 1722   Fax: +61 3 9482 4208; email: *billings@ozemail.com.au*; website: *www.woomb.org*.

Canada: WOOMB, Mrs Lou Specken 1506 Dansey Avenue, Coquitlam B.C. V3K 3J1. NFP Association Alberta, Mrs Gerri Van Der Heuvel, 2405 12th Avenue, South Lethbridge, Alberta, T1K DP4.

England: Billings Family Life Centre, The Basement, 58B, Vauxhall Grove, London SW8 1TB. Tel: 020 7793 0026   Fax: 020 7820 6501.
NAOMI, The Billings Method Reference Centre. C/o 4 Southgate Drive, Crawley, West Sussex RH10 6RP. Tel/Fax: 01444 881 744.

India: SERFAC, P.O. Box 18, Tambaram West, Madras 600-045.

Mexico: WOOMB, J Arturo Amador Hernandez, National Coordinator, J.F. Orozco No 512, Col. San Felipe C.P. 31240, Chihuahua, Chih.

Nigeria: P.L.A.N., HQ (Dr Leonie McSweeney), PO Box 3086, Ibadan, Oyo State.

Slovak Republic: Centrum planovaneho rodicovstva, NsPF D Roosevelta, Namestie L. Svobodu 1, 975 17 Banska Bystrica.

U.S.A.: BOMA-U.S.A., P.O. Box 16206, St Paul, MN 55116. *boma-usa@msn.com*; *www.boma-usa.org*; (001 651 699 8139)

Zimbabwe: Mrs Sybil Gray, PO Box 4024, Bulawayo.

Further reading

The Catechism of the Catholic Church

Humane Vitae	Pope Paul VI	(CTS, London. (Do 411)
Familiaris Consortio	Pope John Paul II	(CTS, London. (S 357)
Letter to Families	Pope John Paul II	(CTS, London. (S 434)
Veritatis Splendor	Pope John Paul II	(CTS, London. (Do 616)
Evangelium Vitae	Pope John Paul II	(CTS, London. (Do 633)

The Catechism of the Catholic Church is not only 'highly recommended', it is *essential reading* for all Catholics who wish to be formed in, and informed by, the authentic teaching of the Church. A complete and unabridged version of the Catechism (mass market edition) is now available from most Bookshops in the U.K. priced at £9.99.

"I should like to close with a brief story. Before the Catechism was published, one of its final drafts was shown to an elderly Bishop, highly respected on account of his erudition, in order to obtain his judgment. He returned the manuscript with an expression of joy. Yes, he said, this is the faith of my mother. He rejoiced to find the faith which he had learned as a child and which had sustained him his whole life long, expressed in its wealth and beauty, but also in its simplicity, and indestructible unity. This is the faith of my mother: the faith of our Mother, the Church. It is to this faith that the Catechism invites us."

(Pope Benedict XVI, when Prefect of the Congregation for the Doctrine of the Faith, concluding his *'Introduction to the Catechism of the Catholic Church'* - Ignatius Press, 1994.)